GW00706122

PENNY

SHARES

MADE SIMPLE

Contents

Why are penny shares so popular?

Investing in Penny Shares is much more exciting than putting your money into an electricity or water company or some other large concern where earnings will only grow at a few per cent each year. In contrast, many Penny Shares have the potential to multiply their profits many times over.

Penny Shares can be classed as any company whose share price is less than £1, although they are just as likely to be shares trading at less than 50p. This means they encompass a wide range of sectors. The only thing they have in common is that they are Penny Shares.

Investors intuitively feel that they are getting more shares for their money. Holding 100,000 shares in a company feels like a significant stake even if 1,000 shares in a larger company is worth the same amount of money.

A few pence on a Penny Share's price will yield a much bigger gain than the same rise on a share price of a few pounds. Each year the best UK Stock Market performers include a large proportion of Penny Shares*.

So what is it about Penny Shares that means they produce such gains? In theory, any company's shares could be classed as Penny Shares. In reality, though,

*SOURCE: Primark DataStream

large companies, such as British Telecom, ICI and Glaxo Wellcome, feel that their size and status warrants a share price expressed in pounds. In practice, then, Penny Shares tend to be smaller companies.

5 reasons for explosive growth in penny shares

According to research by Elroy Dimson and Paul Marsh of the London Business School, smaller companies outperform their larger counterparts nearly every year. The exceptions tend to be during a recession when investors are more likely to stick to less risky, larger companies. Looking over a longer period of time the outperformance is even more marked.

It could be a ground-breaking new product

A Penny Share may have a great new product or service that it is just about to exploit. This could be a newly discovered drug or piece of electronic equipment. It may just be a new way of doing something in an established industry.

Or recovery from a slump

Or it might be that it has been through a tough period of trading but this is now behind it and its fortunes are on the up. This reversal of fortune may not become apparent to the Stock Market immediately and anyone who spots it early can make a great deal of money when the market finally

*SOURCE: DataStream

sits up and takes note.

It's the people that count...

New management may have taken control at a Penny Share company and cleared up the mess left by the previous management. It could be that a particular 'company doctor' famed for turning companies around has taken control.

...Especially if they have a track record

Another possibility is a management team that has been successful at one company and then sold it to embark on a new venture. Knowing the right people to back is important.

Fishing for shells

In other cases, a Penny Share may be a small business with limited prospects but its strong balance sheet might make it a suitable 'shell' company. A 'shell' is a company whose main asset is its Stock Market quote. Unquoted companies looking to gain a quote can find it cheaper and more convenient to 'reverse' into a shell – sell their business for a large stake in the acquiring company – than go through the process of a flotation. If you pick the right Penny Share it could make your fortune.

Of course the flipside of the high rewards on offer is the fact that Penny Shares are generally more risky than larger company shares.

Penny Shares tend to have shorter, and sometimes more patchy, track records. They can be more dependent on one, or a limited number of, products and customers. They can also be more dependent on the UK market than larger companies.

You can reduce risk...

Risk can be reduced by weeding out the companies that are in the poorest financial health. One of these companies may eventually end up a winner but even more of them will go to the wall.

Marketability of Penny Shares can be a problem and this adds to risk. Not only can the difference between buying and selling prices be large in percentage terms but if there is little trading in the shares, the price can move sharply on even the smallest trades.

...By diversifying

It's also best to spread risk when investing in Penny Shares. Don't put all your money into one share just because you feel it will soar. Nothing in life is guaranteed, and no matter how sure you are, there may be unforeseen circumstances. (Investing in a meat supplier with a strong management team may have seemed a good idea at one point but when the BSE scare took hold, no matter how good the company is, it could not do anything about its trading.)

It is a better idea to spread the risk between five to ten companies and invest a similar amount in each. This will allow you to take a high-risk punt if the fancy takes you but means that even if the company goes belly up you will still have other chances to make back your loss.

Essentially, though, assessing Penny Shares is not that different from assessing any other shares. The fundamentals still apply. Penny Shares do not miraculously rise in price just because of their status as Penny Shares. There has to be an underlying business that can expand or a management team that can build up such an operation.

It pays to be selective

Sticking a pin in the Financial Times could sometimes come up with a winner but careful analysis of Penny Shares will give you a much greater chance. Many companies have been Penny Shares all of their Stock Market lives and will probably stay that way because their businesses are going nowhere. The trick is to discover the companies which are going places.

Quality of management is important, as are strong finances, although these count for very little if the company is involved in a stagnating industry. A product or service with growth potential is a big plus point. However, a company may not be involved in a rapidly growing industry but it might just be undervalued compared to similar companies.

Reliable information is the secret to success

Getting information on companies is not always easy. This part of the market is under researched by mainstream stockbrokers. Most of the trades on the Stock Market are in the utilities, ICI or other large companies. Because of this, these companies are followed by a large number of analysts. In contrast, Penny Shares are lucky if they have one analyst researching them – there is just not enough trading in the shares to warrant a larger following.

This is how some Penny Shares with exciting growth prospects can go almost unnoticed. Sometimes there is very little trading in Penny Shares between Stock Exchange announcements. But when they do make an announcement share price moves can be rapid. Even so, the market does not always appreciate the full potential so there is sometimes still time to buy the shares after a share price rise.

Make no mistake, Penny Shares can vary greatly in terms of quality and prospects. You don't want to invest in the·dogs, you want to pick the winners.

This is why having good sources of information is important. The one analyst researching the company is also invariably employed by the company's broker. So don't be surprised if that analyst always has a buy recommendation on the shares no matter what is happening to the business. Independent sources of information can be hard to come by. Large libraries have Extel cards on quoted companies and cuttings services which show recent press comment – but by far the best way to find information is on the internet. Two sites of interest are <www.market-eye.co.uk> and <www.iii.co.uk>. However, there is little in the way of analysis. This is where the *Penny Share Guide*® comes in.

The Dos and Don'ts of Penny Share Investing

Most of what follows is common sense. It is all too easy to lose sight of the basics in the exciting thrills and spills of investing in the Stock Market. But common sense should be the solid basis for all investing. This could mean thinking twice about the hype you may read in the mainstream media or hear from your broker. Always ask yourself if an investment sounds reasonable. Then, and only then, should you invest your hard-earned cash. This amount should never be more than you can afford to lose. You should always take into account that share prices may go down as well as up, even though our Penny Share recommendations are carefully selected to minimise your risk.

Seven Dos

1. Do know what you want from your stockbroker

Before you place an order, make sure you know what you want from your stockbroker. An 'execution-only' stockbroker will provide a 'no-frills' dealing service at comparatively low prices. If you are a cost-conscious investor, happy to make your own buying and selling decisions (with the help of *Penny Share Guide®*) without first consulting a stockbroker, then an 'execution-only' stockbroker could be just right for you.

If you want a stockbroker who will give you additional advice and guidance, you can try a firm of stockbrokers who offer a personal service. But be warned – as a result, their charges are much higher. In this case, try to deal through just one stockbroking firm, who know you and know what you require. Do make sure whoever you speak to understands your aims and has sympathy with the rationale behind your Penny Share investments. That way, you can ensure you have him or a colleague there to act as an extra 'check' on any share. However, try to avoid taking up too much of their time by talking to them for too long on the phone.

Don't let your broker fob you off with hype or jargon. If you do not understand what some financial term or City 'in' slang means, by all means ask them to explain it. And don't give up until you do understand.

Remember: If you are left unclear as to what's going on and why, that's their fault, not yours. Never be embarrassed to ask questions and to go on asking until you get all the information you need.

Note: *Penny Share Guide®* sometimes tips overseas companies traded on the London Stock Market. You should check the stockbroker you choose is prepared to deal for you in this area.

2. Do spread your investments

'Always spread your risk' is a vital safety-sense rule. By spreading your investments, you are spreading your risk. Therefore, the more shares you invest in, the safer you make your portfolio. Invest in two different shares and you halve your risk. Spread it over six different shares and you divide the risk by six.

3. Do always set limits

Set a definite limit on the price you are prepared to pay for your shares, and make it absolutely clear to your broker what that limit is. Never leave your bank or broker to buy shares for you 'at the best price they can find'. All too often, this can mean any price – and they could well be careless because it's your money they're spending, not their own. Refuse to pay high prices which bear no relation to the price quoted in *Penny Share Guide*®. A 10%-15% limit over the recommended price can usually be considered reasonable.

4. Do be patient

Often, a certain Penny Share company may look solid and just right for a new entrepreneur to step in, take over and start up new growth, profits and share price rises. This could happen next week, next month or next year. If and when it does happen, the excitement and the profits will be well worth the wait. But in this case, you have to be prepared to be patient and for it to take time.

5. Do base your investment decisions on sound reasoning

You must remember that you should base your decisions, at all times, on hard facts and figures not your emotions. The trap that many investors fall into is that they begin to make their decisions with their heart not their head. They buy a share and see it perform very well, making them a handsome profit, and so they become emotionally attached to the share. You may see a share that has served you well as an old friend and not want to part company when it's time to sell, but nobody has ever made a fortune on the Stock Market by allowing sentiment to influence their dealings, and neither will you. Don't forget your gains are merely paper profits until you sell your shares. You only bank your profits when you sell your shares.

6. Do set yourself a stop loss

Naturally, you'll want to follow up 'a roll' and squeeze every last drop of profit from your shares. But it's a hard fact of Stock Market life that every share must stop growing at some point – even if this setback is only temporary. So, make sure you set yourself a 'stop loss' safety net below the share price. You'll be told exactly where to set your stop losses in each edition of the *Penny Share Guide®*. As the share price moves up, your stop loss does too, so whatever the share's price, this system is always minimising your losses and maximising your gains. When the share price stops rising and falls back past your safety net, sell quickly to lock in your profit. The

Penny Share Guide® gives you the recommended stop-loss price for every share in the portfolio in every issue.

7. Do be clear about your objectives

Penny Shares include many types of companies – some are solid investment stocks, others are highly speculative shell situations or exploration companies. We always make it clear which category new share recommendations belong in. When we recommend these kind of speculative shares, it is because we calculate that the odds are in your favour. However, remember that, by definition, all speculative shares have a high risk factor, and if you are worried about losing money you should keep sight of your objectives and not allow yourself to be tempted from the security of solid Penny Share investments by the possibility of high rewards from riskier stocks.

Seven Don'ts

1. Don't chase prices up

If *Penny Share Guide®* recommends a share at 10p, and when you come to buy it, you find the price has gone up to 14p, remember that is a 40% increase. You should also remember that the market makers' large research departments study every share tip written up. After any recommendation anywhere, they naturally think everyone who approaches them wants to buy that share. So, of course, they put up the price to try to make a larger profit on all the shares they may hold in that company. But if buyers hold off, the market-makers will have to mark down the price again, in order to attract business. In that way, the Stock Market is no different from any other market.

2. Don't fight the fall

Whatever you may think, if the price of a share keeps on falling against the market trend, it is usually a sign that something is wrong. Take heed of what it's trying to tell you. Whatever you do, don't buy then ... and if you hold any, think seriously about selling them. You cannot afford to be sentimental about your share buys. If a share starts to look bad, don't hang on in there, hoping against hope it will turn itself around. As soon as it breaches the stop loss recommended by the *Penny Share Guide*® – Sell..

3. Don't buy a sinking share

Wait until a share has stopped falling and steadied in price – or has started moving up again for a day or two, before you buy it. If you buy falling shares in the hope, "they can't go any lower – they'll start rising soon", you could get badly burnt. This is the Stock Market equivalent of the old phrase, 'Never catch a falling knife'. In this case, that can be a very useful phrase to remember.

4. Don't put all your eggs in one basket

If you guess correctly, buying just one share in large

amounts might be the way to make your fortune. But if you get it wrong, it could just as easily be the way to lose the lot. So don't, whatever you do, get over-committed to any one share, or sector – ie: don't only buy shares in oil companies or invest in too many building firms. That way, if the price of oil tumbles, or the property market collapses and puts builders out of business, you won't find all or most of your shares are suddenly at risk.

5. Don't forget to keep accurate records

You need to keep accurate, legible, up-to-date records of what you bought, what you sold, and how much money you made. It is far easier to keep accounts as you go along, tallying up at the end of each month, rather than to do it all in a rush before your accounts are due at the end of the tax year, when you may no longer quite remember what you bought, or when you bought it. You will need these records both for yourself, so you can keep a detailed account of which share strategies worked for you and which didn't, and for the tax man, who will demand to see all your accounts at the end of the tax year. Profits you make from shares are liable to Capital Gains Tax. The Capital Gains Tax allowance is £7,200 for the tax year ending April 2001. That means you can make £7,200 worth of Capital Gains for the year before you're subject to taxation. For the tax year ending April 2001 you can shelter up to £7,000 tax-free in an ISA and a further £5,000 per year thereafter.

6. Don't forget to read *Penny Share Guide*®

Penny Share Guide's team of expert researchers, will take the work out of Penny Shares for you. They'll analyse everything which might affect your shares: management track records, past profits, current balance sheets, future prospects and customer profiles. They will also watch and examine general trends, with regard to how they might affect your shares. If crime rates are continuing to rise, *Penny Share Guide*® might decide that it is a good time to tip a company bringing out new security devices. If tension in the Middle East means a rise in the price of oil could be likely, then *Penny Share Guide*® might suggest you should consider buying some shares in a new oil company. Our job is to ask all the questions, study all the figures, and check out all the facts. All you have to do is read our final tips, and enjoy the excitement and the potential profits of this explosive market.

Don't forget to read *Penny Share Guide*® carefully for follow-up news on all our past recommendations – it is one of our strengths that we will continue to follow up our tips until we advise a sale, rather than leaving you stranded, wondering if and when you should sell. Our *Penny Share Guide*® team is there to track your shares' progress for you, so do make use of it to keep up-to-date on how your shares are doing. Remember: every single month you'll be told exactly what to do.

7. Don't deal first thing in the morning or last thing in the evening

There tends to be very little dealing by professional investors from large financial institutions first thing in the morning, say before 10.00am. Whereas, private investors like you tend to place buy or sell orders before going to work. This has the effect of making the market relatively uncompetitive when it first opens. This means that you could wind up paying more for your shares than you need to. It is better to place your orders in the middle of the day when prices tend to be more competitive.

- **Penny Shares Made Simple**

Paying For Shares – Rolling Settlement Systems

Depending on which broker you use, you will either have to pay for your shares immediately, within three days, five days, 10 days, or even 20 days.

On 18 July 1994, the traditional accounting day system of the Stock Market was replaced by a new system of 10-day Rolling Settlement, covering all UK equities (including all Penny Shares). However, it changed yet again on 26 June 1995 to become a five-day Rolling Settlement system. Under this new procedure, you can no longer buy and sell shares during an Account period and then settle on a net basis when it comes to Account day. Instead, every business day is a settlement day rather than the two-to-three weeks of the original system.

Now, each trading day has a corresponding settlement day, five business days (Mon-Fri) later. The trading day is commonly known as T, while the settlement day is T+5.

The Stock Market is moving towards immediate settlement by direct debit. However, this has been slow to arrive in practice. And it is envisaged that there will be a T+3, or three-day rolling settlement system, sometime in the future as we move towards immediate settlement. Sharewise, the execution-only broker recommended by *Penny Share Guide*® still offers T+10. This gives you ten whole days before you have to pay for your shares. The calendar below indicates how the different rolling settlement systems work in practice.

S	M	T	W	T	F	S	
	1	2	3	4	⑤	6	Immediate settlement
7	8	9	⑩	11	⑫	13	T+3
14	15	16	⑰	18	19	20	T+5
21	22	23	24	25	26	27	T+10
28	29	30	㉛				T+20

* 20-day settlement is still available to members of the Fleet Street Investors' Club. Tel: 0113 244 6565.

The Bid/Offer Spread Explained

One aspect of Penny Share investment that is very important for investors to understand is the bid/offer spread and marketability of the shares. This can make investment in Penny Shares more costly than in blue chips and offset part of the greater profits available.

Private investors have to trade in shares through a stockbroker. Most shares are traded by market makers and the stockbroker goes to them with an investor's order. The market makers' job is literally to make a market in a particular share. They are obliged to offer a continuous market in the share and be prepared to buy and sell on demand for any deals up to the normal market size (NMS). This figure does not represent the number of shares you have to buy, but all prices quoted by your broker are firm up to this amount.

Market makers earn their money by quoting a two way price. This consists of a bid price at which they are willing to buy shares and an offer price at which they will sell them.

The spread between the bid and offer prices can vary widely. It can be particularly significant on low price shares. A 5p spread on a share trading at 500p represents only 1% of the share price. Contrast this with a 1p spread on a share trading at 5p. In this case the spread represents a whopping 20% of the share price. This leaves the investor with an immediate 20% deficit on the deal even before taking into account any stockbroker commission and the 0.5% government-imposed stamp duty on purchases.

So what does this mean in practical terms for an investor? A 1p bid/offer spread on a share trading at 5p means that the market maker is willing to sell the shares for 5.5p each or buy them for 4.5p.

Let us assume you decide to buy at this price and a few weeks later the price has risen to 6p. On the face of it this is good news – but greater scrutiny shows it is not quite as good as it seems. If the market maker has maintained the bid/offer spread at 1p it will be willing to sell the shares at 6.5p and buy them at 5.5p.

In other words, despite a 20% rise in the published share price you would only be able to sell the shares for the price at which they were bought. Taking into account other trading costs, you're still in loss.

In practice, the bid/offer spread on Penny Shares is not necessarily 1p – it is just as likely to be 0.5p. There is no hard and fast rule on bid/offer spreads relative to a share price. As share prices rise, spreads of 1p or 2p are not such a problem in percentage terms.

Large spreads are not just confined to Penny Shares. Many high price shares have poor marketability. For instance, Savoy Hotels 'B' shares have been quoted at £30-£35 – a bid/offer spread of £5. Even more marketable higher-priced shares can have spreads of 20p or more.

Bid/offer spreads do not remain constant. Sometimes competing market makers in a share quote different prices. One may quote 9p-10p and another 9.5p-10.5p. The touch, or effective bid/offer spread for a share is based on the best selling and buying prices available in the market at any one time. In this case, the best price you could obtain if selling shares is 9.5p while the cheapest buying price is 10p. This means the touch is 9.5p-10p. This means the bid/offer spread is 0.5p.

The marketability of a share can be affected by the number of market makers it has. The greater the number of market makers, the more liquid the market in the shares is likely to be. As long as a share has two or more market makers it will be quoted on the Stock Market Automatic Quotation system (SEAQ). If it only has one market maker it will be quoted on SEATS (Stock Exchange Alternative Trading System). These shares are more difficult to deal in.

The NMS of the SEAQ-quoted shares is also important. It is based on the average size of deals over the previous 12-month period. Market makers can change their bid/offer spread if an investor wants to buy more shares than the NMS. The higher the NMS, the more marketable a share. In effect, though, it is the equivalent monetary value of the NMS that matters. A Penny Share trading at 10p may have a relatively large NMS of, say, 100,000 but this still only represents £10,000 worth of shares – not an enormous holding.

Don't think that just because a company's shares

are Penny Shares they are automatically less marketable than higher priced shares. In practice, some Penny Shares are traded many times in one day. This can't be said of all higher priced shares. Like some Penny Shares, they may be traded infrequently – in a small number of cases going a week or more between trades.

The monopoly of the market makers has come under threat in recent times. Tradepoint, an order driven system, has set up in competition to the Stock Exchange. The Stock Exchange itself is paving the way for its own order driven system through the launch of Sequence, an intergrated computer system providing trading and information services to market participants.

Order driven trading works by sellers and buyers posting the amount of stock they wish to buy or sell and the price they are willing to pay or sell at. There is no spread on the shares. However, sellers have to wait until a buyer comes along who is willing to pay the required price. This is unlikely to take much time with blue chip companies but where trading is less regular, such as many Penny Shares, it may take some time to match buyers and sellers.

Currently, this order-driven system only operates when buying or selling the 100 largest companies listed on the London Stock Exchange. By definition these FT-SE 100 companies are too big to be of interest to penny share investors looking for explosive growth.

Even under the present trading system, market makers keep very little stock in the less frequently traded companies on their books. This means that it can be difficult to pick up a significant holding in a company. In effect, if a stockbroker wants to pick up a large holding for a client it has to seek out an existing shareholder who is a willing seller.

A share can be described as being marketable if large quantities of shares can be traded without shifting the price. Any trade, however small, can have a disproportionate effect on the price of a share with poor marketability. Many Penny Shares may have major stakes in the hands of a limited number of shareholders who have no intention of selling them. This means that the free float, or number of shares truly available to be traded, is small. This can be a cause of poor marketability and investors should bear this in mind when buying the shares.

Poor marketability can mean that when bad news is announced it can be difficult to sell the shares at anywhere near the quoted price.

The bid/offer spread and lesser marketability of Penny Shares should not put off investors because they know that time after time Penny Share companies top Stock Market performance tables.

- **Penny Shares Made Simple**

The Essential Guide to Stop Loss Strategies

When should you sell your shares? This is a particular poser for Penny Share investors, for these shares often perform best right at the very end of a bull market. Sell too soon, and you risk missing out on the best of the rises. Sell too late, and you may see prices pole-axed before you have a chance to do anything about it – as many investors found to their cost in October 1987.

One solution to the problem is to apply a 'stop loss' to all or some of the shares in your portfolio. A stop loss is a pre-ordained selling point, which is triggered when a share price falls through it, and thus acts as a mechanical aid to selling decisions.

Stop losses are variable, and are set as a percentage of the current share price. At 100p, for example, a typical 10% stop loss would be set initially at 90p (100p-10%). As the price rises, so the stop loss will rise in tandem – in this case, an upward move in the shares to (say) 120p would raise the stop loss to 108p (120-10%). The crucial point to note is that although stop losses can rise, they can never fall. In this case, if the share price were to drop subsequently to 100p, the stop loss would remain at 108p, not fall back to 99p (110p-10%). You'll be told exactly where to set your stop loss in each issue of the *Penny Share Guide*®.

Since a share should be sold automatically if a stop loss is breached, the level at which it is set initially represents the maximum possible loss.

What's the point? In the first place, stop losses ensure that you do not sell shares while they still have upward 'momentum', whatever you come to think of their fundamental investment value. More importantly, they take care of the selling decision – the one which nearly all investors find most difficult. On shares which have risen substantially, greed (for further gain) and fear (of lost profit) are often in keen competition. Conversely, when situations turn sour, many people find it difficult to admit a mistake and cut a loss. This is particularly unfortunate in the Penny Share market – for, as we often point out, a reasonably high proportion of 'dogs' is practically inevitable.

Where should stop losses be set? There is no absolute rule – it depends on what you are trying to achieve, and what sacrifices you are prepared to make. At one extreme, you might set rigid stop losses of 10% for all shares in your portfolio. This would be a relatively sensitive tripwire – you would be protected from significant loss on all your holdings, but you would also find many shares being 'stopped out' on temporary and relatively minor setbacks in the share price. It follows that portfolio turnover would be high, and that several long-term 'big winners' might slip through your fingers. At the other extreme, you might set a very insensitive stop loss at 50% of the share price. This will rarely be triggered, but it does at least ensure that you will salvage something from situations which go badly wrong.

If you decide to set a stop loss, you should act on it – otherwise the whole exercise is pointless. Time and again, investors allow emotion to cloud their judgement. Shares are for selling, as well as buying. The only profits which count are the ones you take, the ones you bank. You know the clichés. They make sense. Nothing matters so much as the cash in your account. Paper profits alone are worthless.

There is just one simple, inflexible rule – never lower the stop loss price. Once you have set the margin, stick to it. As soon as your share hits that stop loss, sell. The essence of the system is that it operates mechanically. It imposes a discipline so many investors lack. We all want to believe we have picked the right share, that it will turn around given a little more time.

All too often, private investors end up doing exactly the opposite of the 'cut your losses, run your profits' rule. They sell winners in order to carry on holding losers. Sometimes it works – sometimes. More often than not, the loser goes lower, while the winner which was sold goes on rising.

The stop loss system is not infallible. There will be times when it prompts you to take a loss on some share just before it turns around and soars ahead. Too bad. But it is right more often than it is wrong, much more often.

No investor gets ten out of ten stocks right. Anyone who gets more right than wrong is doing well – and should make money with a stop loss system.

Long-term investment holdings (and especially income stocks) can live with relatively insensitive stop losses. For short-term speculations – especially if they have already done their stuff – a hair-trigger may be more appropriate. Very 'light' share prices (say those under 10p) may also need fairly wide stop losses, for even if the price is locked in a sideways 'random walk', it will look pretty volatile on a percenatge basis.

Remember: the stop losses suggested in the monthly issues of *Penny Share Guide*® are for your guidance only. If you want to vary them according to your own predictions and/or circumstances – or, indeed, ignore them altogether – that is entirely up to you.

The Essential Guide To Aim and Ofex Companies

As its name suggests, *Penny Share Guide*'s policy has always been to recommend shares with 'light' trading prices. Although the definition of a Penny Share is fluid, we have found in practice that £1 is the most useful cut-off point for new recommendations.

Even at the top of the range, prices are still low enough to be highly attractive to private investors. At the same time, there is plenty of choice: more than enough shares qualify to enable us to sort out the sheep from the goats, and to offer you a wide variety of investment ideas.

We tip recovery stocks, growth stocks, takeover situations, exploration companies – even solid investment stocks which are temporarily down on their luck, or which have unusually low share prices for technical reasons. Even so, we have found that there are two types of company which have particular appeal for many of our readers. One is the very small, very young company which may grow a great deal larger in time – the 'acorn to oak' situation. The other is the 'shell', a quoted company of no importance which is transformed by the injection of new business or new management.

In the past, *Penny Share Guide®* has tipped a great many shells and small growth companies. But the £1 cut-off point has meant that we have also had to allow many tempting investment prospects to escape our net. So when the Alternative Investment Market (AIM) was launched in June 1995, providing a major new venue for small growth companies, we decided we should relax our policy – that we should add a new section to the newsletter to cover all AIM companies regardless of individual share prices. The amount of tradable smaller companies was extended even further in October 1995 with the launch of the off-exchange market, or Ofex, by J P Jenkins. And, if we were going to do that for growth stocks, we saw no reason why we shouldn't add a similar section devoted to shells. The result is that *Penny Share Guide®* has been significantly expanded to give you more investment ideas in areas you find particularly exciting. The purpose of this chapter is to explain what shells, AIM and Ofex companies are, what rewards (and risks) they offer to private investors, and how to go about investing in them to maximum effect.

The Alternative Investment Market

The Stock Exchange provides an organised venue where companies can raise capital from the public, and investors can trade shares between themselves. In the UK, as in other countries where the Stock Market has been at the heart of the capitalist system for centuries, the system works very well. But it has one major flaw. In order for people to invest with confidence, the market has to be strictly regulated. Companies must have an established trading record before they are eligible for a listing, and they must obey strict reporting and other requirements afterwards. The problem is that compliance with the regulations is expensive, putting an intolerable burden on very new and/or very small companies.

Promising companies in this position have always been able to raise capital from the banks and specialist venture-capital institutions. But the mismatch in power means that entrepreneurs usually have to sell their equity very cheaply, and often feel that they are being cheated. At the same time, the private investor – who might well be willing to pay more to get in on the 'ground floor' of fledgling companies – finds himself shut out. The question has always been how to devise a market where shares in small companies can be freely traded, but which strikes a fair balance between the interests of entrepreneurs (who want a reasonable price for their shares) and private investors (who need some protection from charlatans).

An earlier attempt to strike this balance was provided by the Unlisted Securities Market (USM). This was run by the Stock Exchange, and used all the Stock Market's conventional trading mechanisms. To get onto the USM, companies needed only a three-year trading record instead of the usual five; they did not have to release a minimum 25% of their equity; and both the initial entry and later compliance costs were significantly reduced. The USM was seen as the 'junior' market – a staging post on the way to a full Stock Exchange listing. In this respect, it proved highly successful – with several hundred companies earning promotion over the years.

Beyond the USM, even smaller and younger companies could be traded on the OTC (Over-The-Counter) markets. These were essentially unregulated private markets, operating outside the control of the Stock Exchange. Although some OTC companies proved successful, the combination of hard-sell marketing techniques and inadequate supervision meant that too many naive investors were sucked into catastrophic investments. After a brief surge of popularity in the early 1980s, disillusion with the OTC quickly set in. Although a later attempt to establish an orderly 'Third Market' proved abortive, the Stock Exchange allowed market-makers to trade in the shares of unquoted companies under its obscure Rule 4.2. Although this was never entirely satisfactory, it did provide a shadowy market with some element of regulation.

In its heyday, the USM was highly popular with both small companies and private investors alike. But it was overtaken by events when the Stock Exchange reduced its entry requirements for a full listing in order to harmonise with other European Bourses. As a result, the distinction between USM and fully-listed companies (never very great from the investor's point of view) largely disappeared, and many new companies decided to wait an extra year for a full quotation and so cut out the USM stage altogether. At this point, the Stock Exchange decided to create an entirely new junior market – one which could take over the old role of the USM, and at the same time tidy up the market which had grown up under Rule 4.2. After prolonged consultation (and much argument) with interested parties, the Alternative Investment Market (AIM) opened for business in June 1995.

To qualify for the AIM, companies do not need a trading record of any sort. However, they are required to issue a prospectus, produce regular trading statements and disclose price-sensitive information to the Stock Exchange. Above all, they must have a nominated advisor (and, if necessary, a nominated broker). Advisors must be appointed from a register maintained by the Stock Exchange – and it is the advisor, rather than the management, which is held responsible for the company's conduct. If an advisor resigns, a company has three months to find a replacement or else face expulsion from the market. The purpose of this rule is to ensure that no company can be traded on the AIM without being first vetted and then supervised by a responsible party with something to lose. The performance of nominated advisors is monitored, and they can be struck off the register if their misconduct or negligence is held to damage 'the integrity and reputation' of the market.

These rules protect investors from obvious sharks and fraudsters, the bane of unregulated OTC markets. They also guarantee some sort of trading facility. If there is a reasonable number of shares in issue, and there is a market maker conducting two-way business, shares can be bought and sold in the normal way. Otherwise, AIM companies must have a nominated stockbroker whose function is to match bargains and report information to SEATS PLUS – the Stock Exchange Alternative Trading Service.

Acorns to Oaks

The variety of companies quoted on the AIM is immense. It includes small regional brewers, local railways, tightly-controlled family firms – even large but publicity-shy companies. Many of these companies are mature (some are ancient), and have no particular ambition to grow much larger. There is little investment interest in such companies, and *Penny Share Guide*® only deals with them on the rare occasions they are used as shells.

Much more interesting are thrusting little growth companies and start-up situations. These are companies which would normally issue shares to the big venture capital houses, and remain unquoted until they have achieved sufficient size (and a sufficient track record) to seek a full Stock Exchange listing. Such companies can now come to the AIM at a much earlier stage in their development, giving private investors the chance to get in right at the beginning.

This has clear advantages from an investment point of view. Companies, like national economies, have a clearly-defined life cycle. Once they have survived the hazards of extreme youth, they enter a period of very rapid growth. This slows down with the onset of maturity, to be followed by a gradual decline into old age and (eventually) death or trans-formation. In human beings, the life cycle is biologically determined and is thus predictable within well-defined limits. The fate of companies, being commercially determined, is much less certain. Some companies mature quickly, others remain in a growth phase for decades. Even the latter, however, will produce their fastest growth in their earliest years.

Pundits often claim that investment in growth stocks is easy. All the investor has to do is pick a company producing reliable growth, buy its shares, then stick to it like a limpet for years as it puts on weight. This is the 'acorns to oaks' theory – and if the right acorns are selected, there's no doubt that it can produce extraordinary gains. Sainsburys started life in 1869 as a single dairy shop in London. Marks & Spencer traces its origins to 1884, when Michael Marks set up his 'Penny Bazaar' on a trestle table in Leeds' Kirkdale market. Now these two companies are among the mightiest oaks in the forest, and their early shareholders (or at least their heirs) have made a fortune.

The problem, unfortunately, is that a great many other acorns were sown in the late 19th century. As in all periods, many failed to put down roots and remained fallow. Rather more made it to the sapling stage, and some of these will have grown into quite decent trees. Of course, even of those which 'made it', most matured many decades ago – later sinking into decline or suffering absorption into bigger companies through take-over and merger activity.

The truth is that investment in growth companies is trickier than many people suggest. Buy into well-established growth stocks (which are always popular) and you will have to pay a high price. To justify that price, the company will have to continue growing rapidly – for if the growth rate slows, investors will fear that maturity is approaching and the rating of the shares will fall.

The alternative is to invest in fledgling growth companies which have still to prove themselves. These are almost always a long way from maturity, and a relatively high proportion of them are involved at the cutting edge of technological, commercial or social change. As a result, they are often exploiting new growth markets with relatively little competition, and in the early stages are capable of producing explosive growth rates. Get into such situations before the crowd, and they can produce startling profits. As one would expect, the AIM attracts large numbers of such companies, and it is among these that *Penny Share Guide*® concentrates much of its researches.

There is a distinct class of even smaller and younger companies which can be found on the AIM. These are 'start-up' situations – companies with no track record at all, and little more than an invention and/or business plan to their name. From the investor's point of view, this is like getting in on the basement rather than the ground floor – and it should be remembered that although many start-ups succeed, the casualty rate is extremely high. On the whole, we feel that this is an area best left to specialist institutions which can afford to buy into a very wide range of situations. At *Penny Share Guide*®, we prefer to see some sort of track record (however short), and we only recommend start-ups if we feel that they have something exceptional to offer in the way of proven management and/or financial backing.

Even among companies which have got off the ground, the casualty rate is much higher than average. The Stock Exchange is keen to avoid too many embarrassing failures, and the AIM regulations should at least ensure that fraudsters and obvious no-hopers are kept off the market. Even so, there are many natural hazards which fledgling growth companies have to face. The first is competition. Imitation, as they say, is the sincerest form of flattery – and companies which hit on a highly profitable new niche market or business stratagem can be sure that others will try to muscle in on their territory. If the market is big enough, or entry costs are high, or the pioneering company has a sufficient head start, this need not matter. But some growth niches can become overcrowded very quickly, and sometimes the small fry can be scattered if a major company with much greater financial resources decides to enter the market. When IBM trained its immense firepower onto the fast-growing personal computer market in the mid-1980s, many smaller players were ruined overnight.

The second major hazard is management inadequacy. By definition, young companies are run by entrepreneurs – in many cases, by people who have invented a new product or developed a unique service. Entrepreneurs tend to be high on intelligence, imagination, ambition and drive – and in the early stages of a company's life, these qualities may be enough. Later on, they will not be. As companies expand, they need to pay much more attention to managerial and financial controls; to rely on system as well as flair. On the whole, entrepreneurs make poor bureaucrats – and some of them, especially if they have founded the business, find it difficult to delegate. The necessary transition from an entrepreneurial to a more bureaucratic style of management is often mishandled; too many promising companies go bust because they try to expand too quickly and pay insufficient attention to their financial and managerial base.

These hazards exist, but they should not be exaggerated. The majority of entrepreneurs are aware of their managerial limitations, seek advice, and take care to introduce management in depth as their enterprises expand. Most are also thoroughly familiar with the markets they serve, and their companies are small enough (and flexible enough) to take avoiding action when problems loom on the horizon. Well-publicised failures apart, it shouldn't be forgotten that smaller companies in general outperform their larger peers decade after decade. This is not because smaller companies are inherently superior to large ones – many of them are distinctly dull. But the smaller-companies category also includes those expanding very rapidly in new growth markets, and it is these which pull up the averages. Almost by definition, companies of this sort are heavily represented on the AIM.

Given the risks facing all fledgling companies, investors in the AIM cannot expect to win every time. In this sort of market, success depends on achieving a high strike rate. If you have six carefully-chosen shareholdings, you can do very well if you have one big winner, two reasonable performers, two which do nothing and one which is an abject failure. If you hit on two big winners out of the six, you may make extraordinary profits. Remember that the averages work in the investor's favour: the downside on any single share is limited to 100%, while the upside is theoretically limitless. In any particular year, the top performance tables show many shares which have appreciated by several hundred per cent. Almost without exception, these are the shares of very small companies.

The Ofex alternative

Ofex started dealing in shares on 2 October 1995 and was set up by old-City hand John Peter Jenkins. He progressed through his father's stockbroking business – starting as a messenger at 15 and working his way up to a senior partner in 1982. In 1991 he started to trade in smaller company shares as a market maker. JP Jenkin's Ofex market was launched as an arena for dealing in 'unquoted' shares. This market has been subject to some critisism in the past – the main bone of contention being the perception that it's easy for poor quality companies to get a listing because the regulation of this market is looser. But the main beauty of this market is the lower listing and maintainance cost – ideal for small, entrepreneurial businesses – exactly the type of companies the *Penny Share Guide*® recommends. But, despite these critisims, the *Penny Share Guide*'s comprehensive research and analysis will only bring to you the best opportunities existing on this market. You can find Ofex companies' share prices listed in the Financial Times under 'Other Markets'.

The role of *Penny Share Guide*® is to increase the strike rate of readers interested in the AIM and Ofex. Naturally, we look for exciting companies with exceptional potential. But no matter how glamorous a company may seem, we will avoid it if the management seems to be long on big ideas but short on practical common sense – for these are the situations which invariably tempt investors into disaster. We want to see evidence that the management has its feet on the ground; that they have a plausible business plan for turning potential into reality, are aware of the risks as well as the opportunities, and have potential resources of both finance and advice on which to draw.

By weeding out the obvious losers, and concentrating on companies with a real chance of commercial success, we believe we greatly improve the odds in favour of subscribers prepared to act sensibly and buy a reasonable spread of shareholdings. But it should be recognised that AIM investments are at the upper end of the risk/reward spectrum, and that neither we nor anyone else can pick winners every time. Happily, the Government recognises the risks – and as it is keen to encourage private venture capital, it offers a number of tax concessions to compensate for them.

The Tax Breaks

Technically, all shares traded on the AIM are treated just like Ofex shares – they are 'unquoted'.This may seem absurd – all it really means is that they are not formally listed on the Stock Exchange. Even so, the unquoted tag has practical consequences. Certain trust funds are barred from investing in them, and they cannot be incorporated into Isa portfolios. More importantly, it means that they qualify for significant tax concessions.

The most important tax break, at least for bigger investors, is Capital Gains Tax (CGT) roll-over relief. Under the rules, any chargeable gains arising from the sale of shares or any other assets can be deferred if the proceeds are reinvested in unquoted companies. Moreover, investors have three years to make the reinvestment, and can reclaim any CGT already paid provided they meet the deadline. This relief greatly increases the appeal of the AIM for investors who already have a real or potential CGT problem. Quoted investments (or any other chargeable assets) can now be sold, and CGT avoided, by reinvesting the proceeds on the AIM.

Income Tax relief upfront is also available for those who invest through the Enterprise Investment Scheme (EIS) and new Venture Capital Trusts. EIS companies are similar to the old BES trading companies, with the difference that they can be traded on the AIM. Venture Capital Trusts are investment trusts which specialise in unquoted companies, including AIM companies. In both cases, investors can claim lower-rate tax relief (at 20%) up to £100,000 in any single tax year. However, there are two restrictions. Financial and property companies do not qualify, and investments must be held for five years or the relief is forfeited.

Finally, all unquoted companies qualify for Inheritance Tax relief. For those controlling less than 25% of a company (which applies to practically all private investors in AIM companies), tax relief at 50% can be obtained on the value of qualifying assets. Of course you have to be dead to benefit, but this relief will still be of interest to older subscribers who wish to protect their heirs from a big Inheritance Tax bill. In such cases, we strongly advise that both your heirs and your solicitors are made aware of what you are doing.

Make sure you use your Isa allowance

If you're going to maximise your tax-free gains it is important you chose the right Isa. The first decision you need to make is how much you intend to invest in shares. If you're going to invest less than £3,000 in shares you can open a separate Mini Isas for shares and also have separate Mini-Isas for cash and life insurance.

If you intend to invest more than £3,000 in shares you'll have to open a Maxi Isa. Your gains will be tax-free on investments up to the £7,000 limit. You can invest a maximum of £7,000 in shares, cash and life insurance in a Maxi. You will also get a 10% 'tax credit' on share dividends refunded in your Isa. No tax is payable on dividends and interest recieved in Isas.

You must ensure you open the right type of Isa and advice from an Independent Finacial Advisor is essential. You can find a list of qualified Advisors in your area from the address below – and also, from time to time, you'll find Fleet Street Financial Services will bring to you some of the best Isa deals around.

The Society of Financial Advisors
20 Aldermanbury
London
EC2V 7HY
Tel: 020-7417 4419

- **Penny Shares Made Simple**

The Essential Guide To Shell And Reverse Takeovers

Thanks to modern software, it is now easy to identify the best-performing shares over any particular time period. At Fleet Street Publications, we often take a computer printout of the top twenty performers over the previous 12 months, and we have discovered a very curious fact. No matter what time of year we do this exercise, we find that Penny Shares (shares priced at £1 or less at the beginning of the period), account for at least ten of the twenty. Most often, they account for 15 or more. As Penny Shares make up a relatively small proportion of shares quoted on the Stock Market, it is clear that they are massively over-represented among the best performers.

This is no coincidence, although it would be highly misleading to claim that Penny Shares do exceptionally well just because they are priced at less than £1. The real reason is that there is a large area of overlap between shares with a very low share price, and companies which have a very low market valuation. Some of the latter are used as 'shells', and it is these shells which produce the exceptional gains. Since a great many shells are also

Penny Shares, we have always paid close attention to them in *Penny Share Guide®*. However, there are also numerous exceptions. With the introduction of our shell section, *Penny Share Guide®* is now able to investigate all shells without worrying about share-price levels.

What Shells Are and How They Work

A shell is best defined as a trivial business which is taken over and transformed into something much more significant. One of Britain's largest companies, BTR-Siebe, started life as a shell in the 1960s, since when they have grown into huge multinational con-glomerates of global importance. Obviously, shareholders who have stuck with them throughout this process have made massive profits. But it is not necessary (or even desirable) to hold shell investments for such protracted periods. By far the best gains come in the early stages of a shell operation. Once a shell has been transformed, it becomes a company much like any other.

Before they are activated, shells are almost the exact opposite of brand-new growth companies. Some of them are ancient, some relatively recent – but what they have in common is the fact that they represent the remains (or shells) of companies which were once of much greater importance. What usually happens is that a company gets into deep trouble through bad luck or bad management. Its debt spirals out of control, and as its survival becomes questionable, its share price collapses. At this point, the company is usually described as a 'busted recovery stock'. Some go bankrupt; others eventually manage to haul their way back to prosperity – usually under new management.

When companies are on their uppers, it is quite common for City shareholders and the banks to kick out the old management and install a 'company doctor' in its place. The company doctor will only rarely have a long-term interest in the business. His role is to salvage what he can – and to that end, he will slash costs and sell off assets until he has restored his charge to a modicum of financial health. At the end of this radical surgery, the company should at least be viable, but there may be precious little left of the business. The most valuable asset most shells possess is their Stock Exchange quotation.

That may seem very intangible – quoted or not, a sweetshop is only a sweetshop. In fact, a quoted sweetshop is potentially much more valuable. Owners of private businesses who want to go public can often do so more quickly (and more cheaply) by 'reversing' into a shell company, obtaining a back-door quote in the process. In this case, an unquoted chain of newsagents might be injected into the quoted sweetshop, instantly transforming the business. This is achieved through the mechanism of the 'reverse takeover' – a case of a sprat swallowing a whale. The shell company pays for its acquisition by issuing shares to the vendor, who then takes control of the combined business. Reality is usually more complicated than this simple illustration suggests; shell operations are often accompanied by a financial restructuring of greater or lesser complexity. Even so, the essential principle remains the same. Any company which is subjected to a reverse takeover is a new issue in all but name.

Another type of shell operation occurs when a new management team is injected into the company. In this case, the idea is not to acquire a quote for a pre-existing private business, but to use it to build an entirely new one. Quoted companies can issue shares to raise cash or make acquisitions. So long as there is a ready market for this new equity (and for high-powered management teams, there will nearly always be an enthusiastic band of City supporters), it is quite possible to build up a company from nothing very quickly. This second approach – using a shell as an acquisition vehicle – is in fact much more common than the reverse takeover, and is worth examining more closely.

Growing Shells Through Acquisition

New management rarely moves into a shell 'on spec'. Merchant banks, which are the City's business brokers, put would-be entrepreneurs in touch with suitable shell prospects and arrange any financial restructuring which may be necessary. In this, they usually work closely with a firm of stockbrokers, which will find backers for the new shell vehicle from among their clients. These are the people (individuals or small institutions) who stump up the cash required to buy control of the shell, and to fund any financial restructuring which may be needed. As they become sizeable shareholders in the process, they obviously have a vested interest in the success of the venture. In the early stages, they can normally be relied on to provide additional capital as and when required.

The permutations on this theme are endless. But in essence, a shell is activated when it is taken over by new management with access to City finance. The new team may, or may not, have any interest in developing the original business. If not, they will try to plump it up with a view to sale at some future point, but in any case, their main efforts will be devoted to expansion through the acquisition of other businesses. Finance for the first deal is usually raised through a rights issue to existing shareholders. Thereafter, other techniques may be employed. Shells are often in the business of acquiring management expertise as well as new operations, so if the owner of an acquired business is to become part of the management team, he may accept payment for his company in shares. Sometimes, merchant banks or stockbrokers can arrange a 'vendor placing' with their clients. In this case, payment for the acquisition is made in shares to the vendor, who sells them on to willing shareholders for cash. However it is done, the shell company is exploiting its quote by issuing paper in return for real business assets. In the process, it can grow rapidly in size, even though its financial resources may be extremely limited.

In theory, any quoted company can do this. In practice, it can only be done if there is a ready market for the company's paper. For the first couple of deals, as we have seen, a shell company can usually rely on its original backers. But as it gets bigger, and its capital needs increase, it will require a bigger pool of potential investors. To interest other investors – to give its City advisors a story to sell – it will have to prove that it can produce results.

Results, in this context, means growing earnings-per-share (EPS). On the face of it, a shareholder in a company which is growing rapidly in size (and producing much higher profits as a result), must be onto a good thing. That is a fallacy. If a company is issuing shares to acquire businesses, its capital is expanding as well as its assets. If both are expanding at the same rate, shareholders are no better off than before. If capital is expanding faster than profits, they are actually worse off. To give a very simplistic example, imagine that you own 1,000 shares in a company and that this gives you 1% of the equity. If the company makes profits of £100,000, your share (1%) is £1,000. Now assume that the company issues shares to make acquisitions, doubling its capital and profits in the process. Your share will now be 0.5% of profits of £200,000 – still £1,000. If the company makes profits of £180,000, it can boast a profit increase of 80%, but its original shareholders will not be impressed. In this case, your share of the profits (0.5% of £180,000) would have fallen to £900.

It cannot be stressed often enough that profits by themselves mean nothing. It is only after a company's earnings have been reduced to a per share basis that they give a reliable indication of progress – and it is the price/earnings or p/e ratio (a figure achieved by dividing earnings-per-share into the share price) which is by far the most important investment yardstick. That applies to all companies, but it is particularly important to remember when a company's share capital is constantly expanding.

A successful shell produces value for its shareholders by growing earnings faster than its capital – indeed, so far as the Stock Market is concerned, this is the reason for its existence. The shell achieves this in part by 'adding value' to its acquisitions – by offering stronger management, benefits of scale and other improvements which boost profitability. But in the early stages, at least, it can also increase earnings rapidly through the takeover process itself. This trick is achieved by using expensive shares to make inexpensive acquisitions.

This is best illustrated by another simplified example. Assume that a company with a market value of £5m is making profits of £200,000. Allowing for tax, this company is trading on a p/e ratio of 38, which is extremely high. Its acquisition targets will be on a more normal p/e of about 10 – in other words, it should be able to take over another company making profits of £200,000 for about £1.3m. If it can issue £1.3m-worth of its own (very expensive) shares to make this acquisition, it will immediately enhance its own value. Before the deal, there was a £5m company making profits of £200,000. After the deal, there is a £6.3m company making profits of £400,000. In other words, profits (and earnings) have doubled, but the share capital has increased by only 26%.

The longer a shell company can maintain a high share price, the more often it can repeat this trick. As a result, it can make very rapid progress – and do extremely well for shareholders who get in early. However, as it gets bigger, it will need more and bigger investors to absorb the new shares it is issuing. Before long, these will have to be found among smaller City investment institutions, and later among their bigger colleagues. Quite when a shell ceases to be a shell is another one of those things which has has never been properly defined. In our view, it is when more than 50% of the shares are held by institutional investors. At this point, the company's behaviour will have to be more restrained, and it is better described as a 'mini-conglomerate'.

Investing in Shells

There are various ways investors can choose to play the market in shells. The first is to buy into companies which are good shell prospects – companies with a very low market capitalisation, not much of a business and a relatively 'clean' (ie, debt-free) balance sheet. This is a game for people with patience, who don't mind waiting for the fish to bite. At *Penny Share Guide*®, we generally prefer to have something more tangible to go on, although we occasionally look at small groups of promising shell prospects for readers who like to lock away 'sleepers' in the bottom drawer.

It is more productive, we feel, to wait until a new management team has moved into a shell company. In such cases, investors can at least be sure that major developments will follow, although the precise direction the company will take may still be unclear. What we usually look for here is a gross mismatch between the size of the company and the strength of its new management. It often happens, for example, that managers who have previously run major divisions of giant multinationals will take over a shell in order to run their own show. In such cases, it is a reasonable bet that they will not be content for long to manage a tiny business they could run in their sleep. Except in extremely bearish conditions, it is also a fair bet that they will have no trouble finding enthusiastic backers in the City. Although investors who buy into shells at this stage have to take a great deal on trust, we feel that the odds are definitely in their favour.

A third approach is to wait until the shell company already has an acquisition or two under its belt. This is particularly suitable in cases where the new management team does not have much of a track record, or the shell company itself was in a bit of a mess and in need of sorting out. In such cases, we think it is better to wait until the new team can demonstrate that it has the managerial and deal-making skills to make a success of the situation.

As we have seen, shell companies can make more rapid progress if they can keep their shares relatively expensive. To do that, they need to keep the confidence of the market, and to earn a reputation which ensures they can continue to attract new investors. This is more difficult than it looks. A shell company which buys a lemon, or issues too many shares in return for too little growth in earnings-per-share, can lose its premium rating very quickly. Some companies also manage to queer their pitch by bungling their public relations – for example, by telling their shareholders or stockbrokers that they are going to do one thing, and then doing something completely different. Experienced investors have seen too many little acquisition vehicles go wrong as a result of inordinate ambition, and tend to be somewhat sceptical as a result. If the management of a shell company gets a reputation for unreliability, its support will begin to evaporate and the share price will sink.

At *Penny Share Guide*®, we see our main task as identifying shells for our readers among companies which are too small to attract much (if any) attention from City analysts or the mainstream financial press. As with AIM companies, however, we also use our experience to try to sort out the sheep from the goats. We want to see a coherent and plausible corporate strategy, and we greatly prefer it if strong resources of City advice and financial backing are already in place. Above all, we take a view on management quality and intentions. Some entrepreneurs are wholly committed to growing earnings-per-share, and are well aware that this is the yardstick by which they will be judged. Others, we suspect, are simply empire-builders – in the business of making acquisitions for their own personal aggrandisement. It is these latter which will surely fail, and we do our best to weed them out. This requires judgment on our part, and in the nature of things we cannot always be right. But subscribers who buy into shell situations on *Penny Share Guide*® advice can be sure that they have been properly screened by people with the necessary expertise and experience, and its not often that we allow ourselves to be taken in.

- **Penny Shares Made Simple**

Advice For New Investors

If you have never invested in the Stock Market before, or are very new to the game, there are various pitfalls you should be aware of. The most dangerous is over-confidence, coupled with over-ambition. It is very easy to leaf through old copies of investment magazines, and to convince yourself that you would have invested in the big winners and avoided the big losers. The trouble is that we could all be billionaires with the benefit of hindsight. The future, unlike the past, is an open book – anticipating future trends in share prices is an uncertain business. Both mistakes and accidents are inevitable, and it is not much better to accept in advance that this is so, than to find out the hard way. The name of the game, as we have said before, is to achieve a good strike rate; to ensure that your successes outweigh your failures. On shells and AIM companies, the upside potential greatly outweighs the downside (which has an absolute limit of 100%), so the odds are in your favour if you have access to good advice. On the other hand, the onus is on you to invest sensibly.

Investing sensibly does not mean, as some conservative pundits insist, that you must confine yourself to big and boring shares like ICI or British Telecom. If security is all you want, you can achieve it much more efficiently through unit or investment trusts. At *Penny Share Guide®*, we assume that our readers want to take a much more adventurous approach to the Stock Market. That said, there is still a big difference between investing aggressively and pure gambling. Penny Shares in general – and AIM companies and shells in particular – are near the top end of the risk/reward spectrum. That means it is absolutely essential to spread risk by buying a range of investments. If you have only £3,000 to invest, you should buy at least six shareholdings worth £500 each (or even eight worth around £400 each), not put all your money on the one situation you think is the most promising. It may take time to build such a 'portfolio', but with the advent of discount brokerage it is now quite feasible for small investors to do so. We can offer you an introduction to Sharewise, which charges a minimum commission of £15 per transaction (the Government also takes 0.5% in Stamp Duty), making small holdings cost-effective.

We do not give this advice because it is the conventional wisdom, or because we are obliged to do so by the regulators. We give it because: a) it happens to be true, and b) we have a vested interest in our subscribers investing realistically. The last thing we want is for you to take a big gamble, lose a lot of money, become disenchanted with the Stock Market, then blame us and cancel your *Penny Share Guide®* subscription. You should remember that no matter how perfect any particular share may seem, it is always vulnerable to unexpected developments.

We cannot, and do not, pretend that all the shares

we recommend will be big winners, or that there will not be the occasional flop. We can identify companies for you which have good management, good ideas and sound finances – in short, companies with everything going for them. But at the end of the day, we cannot manage the business ourselves, and we cannot force other investors to come in and drive up the share price. If you buy a decent spread of shares, you may not hit the jackpot, but you can realistically expect to increase your investment capital very substantially over time. That is the objective we are in business to help you achieve.

- **Penny Shares Made Simple**

Glossary

Advisory Broker – A stockbroker who offers investment advice but leaves the final investment decision to the investor (see also execution-only broker and discretionary broker).

Alternative Investment Market (AIM) – The London Stock Exchange's new market for smaller companies. The criteria for gaining a quotation in this market are not as strict as those for a full listing.

Bear – An investor who thinks the market will go down (see also bear market, bull and bull market).

Bear Market – A market where the index is falling (see also bear, bull and bull market).

Bid – The price a market maker will pay for a share (see also offer, bid/offer spread and mid-price).

Bid/Offer Spread – The difference between the bid and offer price (see also bid, offer and mid-price).

Blue Chip Companies – Well established companies with a high market capitalisation.

Bourse(s) – A generic name for the stock exchanges of continental Europe.

Broker – (see stockbroker.)

Bull – An investor who thinks the market will go up (see also bear, bear market and bull market).

Bull Market – A market where the index is rising.

Capital Gains Tax (CGT) – You are currently allowed to make £7,100 before you become liable for CGT. Thereafter, tax is levied at the highest rate of income tax you pay.

Crest – The Bank of England's new paperless share settlement system.

Discretionary Broker – A stockbroker who has the 'discretion' to buy shares on an investor's behalf and manage the investor's portfolio (see also advisory broker and execution-only broker).

Dividend – The part of a company's profit which is distributed to shareholders.

Earnings – The net profit of a company that is distributed to its shareholders.

Earnings Per Share (EPS) – Net profit divided by the number of ordinary shares.

Entrepreneur – Someone who by risk and initiative attempts to make profits.

Equity – Basically, ordinary shares.

Execution-Only Broker – A stockbroker who merely carries out a transaction on the investor's behalf without offering advice (see also advisory broker and discretionary broker).

Extel Cards – Index cards which give details on individual companies. You may be able to request these at larger libraries.

Flotation – When a company first issues shares on the Stock Exchange.

FT Actuaries All-Share Index – Covers all shares on the London Stock Exchange and sub-divides them into 40 sectors.

FT-SE 100 Index – An index of the top 100 companies listed on the London Stock Exchange. It is also known as the 'Footsie' and is the principal index for the price of shares quoted on the London Stock Exchange – these are generally regarded as blue chip stocks.

FT-SE Indices – These indices measure the performance of a basket of shares. They are compiled by the London Stock Exchange in conjunction with the *Financial Times* and The Institute and Faculty of Actuaries. They are the FT-SE 100, FT-SE Mid-250, FT-SE SmallCap, FT-SE Actuaries 350, FT-SE Actuaries All-Share, FT-SE Actuaries Fledgling, FT-SE Actuaries Higher Yield, FT-SE Actuaries Lower Yield, FT-SE Eurotrack 100 and FT-SE Eurotrack 200.

FT-SE SmallCap – A measure of the collective performance of smaller companies, many of which are Penny Shares.

Fundamentals – The underlying financial condition of a company based on its actual earnings, assets and dividends.

Gearing – A company's debt expressed as a percentage of its equity capital. High gearing means debts are high in relation to capital.

Going Public – (see flotation.)

Index – A measure of a basket of shares (see FT-SE Indices).

Institutional Investors – Basically, the pension funds and insurance companies who own the majority of quoted shares.

Isa – Individual Savings Account, the tax free wrapper replacing Personal Equity Plans.

Liquid – A market with a lot of buyers and sellers. This makes dealing easy and usually means a narrow bid/offer spread.

Market Makers (MM) – The middlemen prepared to buy and sell shares. They provide liquidity to the market and determine the bid/offer spread.

Mid-Price – A price half-way between the bid and the offer price. You cannot actually buy or sell at this price but it is generally used to indicate value and movement in share listing (eg those found in the 'Companies and Markets' section of the *Financial Times*).

New Issue – Shares coming onto the Stock Exchange for the first time.

Nominated Advisor – A London Stock Exchange approved advisor for AIM companies.

Nominee Accounts – An account where a person or company holds shares on behalf of an investor.

Normal Market Size (NMS) – The SEAQ classification system that replaced the old alpha, beta, gamma system. NMS is a value expressed as a number of shares used to calculate the minimum quote size for each security.

Ofex – the unquoted market for smaller companies

ran by JP Jenkins.

Offer – the price the market maker will offer you for your share.

Offer for Sale – New issues made available to private investors and advertised in the national press.

Ordinary Shares – The most common form of share. Holders receive dividends which vary in amount in line with the profitability of the company and recommendation of directors. The holders are the owners of the company.

Penny Shares – Shares valued at less than £1.

Personal Equity Plan (PEP) – Allows tax benefits on share investment.

Personal Investment Authority (PIA) – The regulator of financial advisors. It is also the authority that regulates the advice we give you in the *Penny Share Guide*®.

Portfolio – An investor's collection of shares.

Price/Earnings Ratio (P/E or PER) – Current share price divided by the company's last published earnings per share (EPS).

Privatisation – The process of converting former state-run companies into public limited companies (plcs). They are generally new issues made available directly to private investors as 'offers for sale'.

Prospectus – New issues of shares from a company must, by law, be accompanied by a detailed document.

Public Limited Company (plc) – A company whose

shares can be traded freely on the Stock Market.

Rights Issue – When an existing plc issues new shares. They are offered to existing shareholders in proportion to their existing holding.

Stock Exchange Automatic Trading System (SEATS) PLUS – A trading service for listed companies whose turnover is too small to qualify for the market making system. It is part of the London Stock Exchange's Sequence programme.

Sectors – Companies quoted on the London Stock Exchange are subdivided into 40 sectors by industry type.

Securities and Investment Board (SIB) – The chief regulator of the financial world. Introduced under the Financial Services Act in the 1980s, it oversees all the self-regulatory organisations in the UK financial world, eg the PIA.

Sequence – The London Stock Exchange's integrated computer system providing trading and information services to market participants.

Sharecall Directory – A FREE 60-page fact-packed directory giving you instant telephone access to the real-time share price of every company quoted on the London Stock Exchange. With calls costing just 50p per minute it is the cheapest way of assessing the real-time value of your Penny Share companies.

Shell Companies – Inactive companies with Stock Market quotations. They can be reversed into by more dynamic companies looking for a cheap entry to the

Stock Market.

Spread – The difference between a market maker's bid and offer price. This spread is greater, in percentage terms, when dealing in Penny Shares (see also bid, offer, bid/offer spread and mid-price).

Stamp Duty – A government tax levied on the purchase of shares. The current rate is 0.5%.

Stockbroker – A member of the London Stock Exchange who provides advice and/or dealing services to investors.

Stock Exchange Automated Quotations (SEAQ) – The dealing and price service introduced on the deregulation of the Stock Market or Big Bang. It is a continuously updated computer database containing price quotations and trade reports in UK securities. SEAQ carries the market makers' bids and offers for UK securities and is part of the London Stock Exchange's Sequence programme.

Stop Loss – A method of minimising potential losses. You place a limit (somewhere between 8% and 15% below the purchase price of your share. If the share falls to this level you then sell to minimise your loss. You can also have a trailing stop loss. This means adjusting your stop loss limit as a share price rises.

Touch – The best bid and offer prices available from market makers.

Trading – The buying and selling of shares.

Unlisted Securities Market (USM) – A forerunner of the AIM.

Warrant – A long-term option to buy shares. These are offered to existing shareholders initially but can also be traded on the Stock Market.

Yield – Annual income from a share based on its current market share.

The Penny Share Guide® advantage . . .

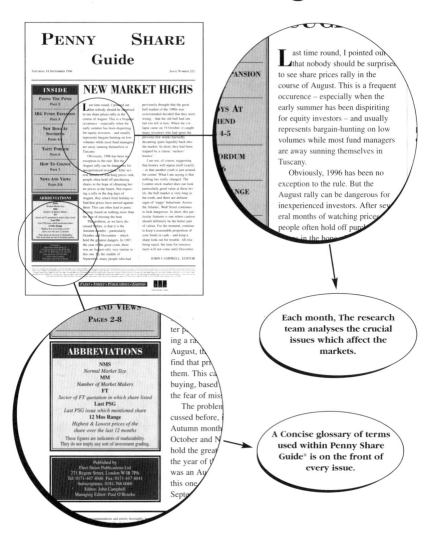

PENNY SHARE Guide

SATURDAY 14 SEPTEMBER 1996   ISSUE NUMBER 225

INSIDE

PAYING THE PIPER
Page 2

IRG FUNDS EXPANSION
Page 3

NEW BOYS AT
SOUTHEND
Pages 4-5

TASTY PORTFOLIO
Page 6

HOW TO CHANGE
Page 7

NEWS AND VIEWS
Pages 2-8

ABBREVIATIONS

NEW MARKET HIGHS

Last time round, I pointed out that nobody should be surprised to see share prices rally in the course of August. This is a frequent occurrence – especially when the early summer has been dispiriting for equity investors – and usually represents bargain-hunting on low volumes while most fund managers are away sunning themselves in Tuscany.

Obviously, 1996 has been no exception to the rule. But the August rally can be dangerous for inexperienced investors. After several months of watching prices sink, people often hold off purchasing shares in the hope of obtaining better prices in the future. Not expecting a rally in the dog days of August, they return from holiday to find that prices have moved against them. This can often lead to panic buying, based on nothing more than the fear of missing the boat.

The problem, as we have discussed before, is that it is the Autumn months – particularly October and November – which hold the greatest dangers. In 1987, the year of the great crash, there was an August rally very similar to this one. By the middle of September, many people who had

previously thought that the great bull market of the 1980s was overextended decided that they were wrong – that the old bull had one last run left in him. When the collapse came on 19 October, it caught many investors who had spent the previous few weeks hurriedly decanting spare liquidity back into the market. In short, they had been trapped by a classic 'suckers' bounce'.

I am not, of course, suggesting that history will repeat itself exactly – or that another crash is just around the corner. What I am saying is that nothing has really changed. The London stock market does not look particularly good value at these levels, the bull market is very long in the tooth, and there are definite signs of 'toppy' behaviour. Across the Atlantic, Wall Street continues to look dangerous. In short, this particular Autumn is one where caution should definitely be the better part of valour. For the moment, continue to keep a reasonable proportion of your funds in cash – and keep a sharp look-out for trouble. All else being equal, the time for reinvestment will not come until December

JOHN CAMPBELL, EDITOR

FLEET · STREET · PUBLICATIONS · LIMITED

AND VIEWS
PAGES 2-8

ABBREVIATIONS

NMS
Normal Market Size
MM
Number of Market Makers
FT
Sector of FT quotation in which share listed
Last PSG
Last PSG issue which mentioned share
12 Mos Range
Highest & Lowest prices of the share over the last 12 months
These figures are indicators of marketability.
They do not imply any sort of investment grading.

Published by
Fleet Street Publications Ltd
271 Regent Street, London W1R 7PA
Tel: 0171-447 4040 Fax: 0171-447 4041
Subscriptions: 0181-768 0080
Editor: John Campbell
Managing Editor: Paul O'Rourke

Last time round, I pointed out that nobody should be surprised to see share prices rally in the course of August. This is a frequent occurrence – especially when the early summer has been dispiriting for equity investors – and usually represents bargain-hunting on low volumes while most fund managers are away sunning themselves in Tuscany.

Obviously, 1996 has been no exception to the rule. But the August rally can be dangerous for inexperienced investors. After several months of watching prices sink, people often hold off purchasing shares in the hope

Each month, The research team analyses the crucial issues which affect the markets.

A Concise glossary of terms used within Penny Share Guide® is on the front of every issue.

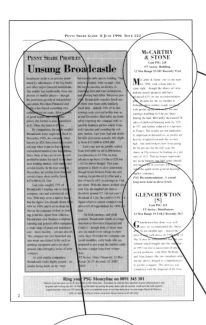

McCARTHY & STONE

Last PSG 218
FT Sector: Building
12 Mos Range 53-101 Recently 91xd

McCarthy & Stone, one of our naps for 1994, took a long time to right – though the shares are ready progress and ha...

Key facts concerning a recommendation are shown at the beginning of each item. *FT Sector*, for example, lists where the company can be found in the *Financial Times*.

PENNY SHARE PROFILES

Unsung Broad

Instalment credit is an activity dominated by subsidiaries of the big banks and other major financial institutions. The market has traditionally been suspicious of smaller players – though the persistent growth of independent specialists Provident Financial and Cattle's has forced something of a think in recent years. After a series ... results and rising share ... er is now capi...

between its ... turn is certai... the key to s... matching de... and limiting... sible, Br... to-three... fixed...

New buy recommendations are clearly highlighted in tinted boxes. Penny Share Guide® also highlights exciting shell opportunities and the dynamic Alternative Investment Market (AIM).

...ontinues.

G Recommendation: A sound long-term hold at these levels.

GLENCHEWTON [S]

Last PSG 215
FT Sector: Distributors
12 Mos Range 19.5-64.5 Recently 56.5

Glenchewton has done very well since we recommended the shares at 26.5p ten months ago – indeed the ... is now well above its 1994 ... ...be remembered...

Each recommendation is updated in the light of news that affects the share price.

Notes

Notes

Notes

Notes

Notes